T

E.

Version 1.1 June 2011
ISBN 978-1461198550

The Flowing River is published by, and is a discipleship
curriculum of the International School of the Bible,
Marietta, GA, U.S.A.
info@isob-bible.org   www.isob-bible.org

Cover art by Tracey Diaz

Table of Contents

The Flowing River
Introduction

Have you ever felt like your life is a waste, a cycle of work and play and activities that have no real value except to help you survive and maybe, just maybe, have a little enjoyment? Have you ever been so desperate just for survival that you did not know where to turn? You look at some people who are prosperous and you are convinced that you could never do that because they are much more talented, gifted, educated, or blessed.

People are really hurting.

Some cannot pay their bills, others have received a bad doctor's report, some have children who have gone astray, and perhaps others have families that are falling apart. We need to be able to know how to cooperate with God through the blood covenant lifestyle so that we can make it in this life, between now and the time we leave this body and go to Heaven.

When Jesus came into my life in 1979 I was in that group of desperate people defined above. Then He came crashing in with an awesome presence that radically changed my entire life, my thinking, my priorities, my emotions, everything. Experiencing His presence meant everything to me. I "saw" Jesus; I could hear His voice. However from time to time I could not find that place of intimacy. That is when I discovered that the Old Testament Tabernacle, that one in the Wilderness, the desert, was my pattern for intentionally making contact with the Creator of all, Jesus, the Father and the Holy Spirit, three in one!

This booklet is a portion of my book, Grow or Die. What I have written in it has been instrumental in the transformation of my life and in the lives of a multitude of people around the world in many languages since 1998. It is a picture of how, even in our human imperfection, we can be "perfect" with God and pleasing to Him.?"

The Flowing River is an invitation to experience the life of God in you, granting you joy and the abundant life. You will experience God speaking to you. As you hear His voice He will bring faith and hope for the future and healing for your past.

Hearing God's voice is the first step into a life that not only will give you peace and purpose, but also will put you on the path which will allow God to become your provider.

Life not religion.

We are saved, set free from bondage, delivered from danger, by the life of God moving into our being.

Romans 5:10 says:

"10 For if when we were enemies we were reconciled to God through the death of His Son, much more, having been reconciled, we shall be saved by His life."

Many people feel that God saves us by Jesus' sacrifice on the cross as an atonement and forgiveness for our sins. While that was a key element in the process, the forgiveness of our sins simply made it possible for God to cleanse us so that He could enter into our being with His life, the life of the Almighty Creator.

This is what I call, "Return to normal." God created Adam from the dust and then moved in to inhabit him. Adam did not keep his free will towards that union, but rather declared his independence, which made it necessary for God to move out. Now Jesus gives us an opportunity to be normal again, a human being filled with the Holy Spirit of God.

However, many Christians only believe and know about the historic Jesus, the one that died on the cross 2,000 years ago, and they have never experienced His life, even though His life may have been there in them all the while. Or perhaps others have only heard about Christianity and Jesus and never really experienced any of it at all.

Others perhaps have had the blessing of the life of God and His presence at some time in their lives, but the daily grind, the cares of this life and maybe even sin has darkened their experience.

The Flowing River is an invitation to experience the life of God in you, granting you joy and the abundant life. You will experience God speaking to you, hearing His voice which will bring faith and hope for the future.

The life of God in you can raise the dead things in your life.
I was sitting talking to the Lord on Good Friday, pondering, with some fear, how in the world was I going to handle this "dead thing" in my life.

He asked me a question. "Larry, do you remember when your business died in 2000?" "Yes Lord," I said. He said, "Are you glad it died?" "Oh yes," I said, "Because when it was resurrected it was 100 times better than before it died." He said, "Larry, there is not any dead thing that I cannot resurrect."

I started crying, then laughing with the joy of the Lord. I was laughing at how I can be at peace and relax no matter what dead thing was giving me a hard time today. Why? Because Jesus would resurrect it and it would be 100 times better, and I would look back and be glad that I had experienced that dead thing.

This book will help to equip you for resurrecting dead things in your life.

However, you must live the overcoming lifestyle. You must take up your cross to deny your flesh nature the opportunity of taking over and stealing your resurrection. You must use discipline to keep up your relationship skills with God. You do that by continually taking up the cross of your fleshly will, mind and emotions; saying no to them.

Then the resurrected Jesus inside of you can prevail and resurrect all the dead things in your life

Another benefit is taking the spoils of the enemy. As you overcome, you will not only receive the benefits in your own life, but you will be overcoming an enemy that has others in bondage as well, and your resurrection will set others free, just as Jesus' did!

On your Good Friday when all you can see is death, start laughing at Satan and start praising God because you know for sure that the resurrection of Easter is coming soon. You can relax while you are in the grave.

We are the Temple of God,
1 Corinthians 3:16 says,

"16 Do you not know that you are the temple of God and that *the Spirit of God dwells in you?"*

If we are God's Temple, then we carry within us the Ark of the Covenant which resides inside the Holy of Holies, and which was in the Tabernacle in the Wilderness and the Temple in Jerusalem. The Old Testament Tabernacle was the Temple during the Israelite's exodus from Egypt to the Promise land as they passed through the wilderness and desert. Of the three major compartments in the Tabernacle, the Holy of Holies is where the presence of God actually dwelt at that time. We will see how we can enter the Holy of Holies now and engage personally with God in His intimate presence.

When we take time to adjust ourselves, and our relationship to the Lord, according to the pattern of the Tabernacle, we put ourselves into a position of intimate fellowship with Jesus and give Him what He needs, and desires, to supply all of our earthly needs. Actually the supply of our earthly needs are simply a by-product of what really pleases Him, and that is to be in intimate closeness to Him and to allow Him to glorify Himself through us to others and to a lost world.

A walk through the Tabernacle is all about the "prosperity of our soul," as described by John in 3 John 1-4, which says,

"1 THE ELDER, To the beloved Gaius, whom I love in truth:

2 Beloved, I pray that you may prosper in all things and be in health, just as your soul prospers.

3 For I rejoiced greatly when brethren came and testified of the truth that is *in you, just as you walk in the truth.*

4 I have no greater joy than to hear that my children walk in truth."

When our soul prospers, our will, mind and emotions, it is rightly aligned to God, and our outward circumstances will begin to prosper in all areas of our lives. Soul prosperity is simply allowing the life of Jesus free reign to live His life in us. That is what the Flowing River is all about, coming into His Holy of Holies, so that we "see" and hear Jesus in ultimate intimacy. Our part of enabling Him to live His life in and through us it to "take up our cross." That is to say no to our carnal will, mind (thinking) and emotions. When we do that we give freedom to Christ to live His life in us.

Certainly prosperity as defined in true New Testament terms is different for everybody, and its process does not exclude trials and sufferings, which normally are a part of the fruit bearing process.

New Testament prosperity is only realized in resurrection. Jesus prospered when He was raised from the dead. Only then did He defeat Satan. It is the same with us. True prosperity comes only after our afflictions, tribulations and suffering; then we are granted the resurrection, which not only defeats those enemies in our realm, but also takes their spoils in other realms and sets others free.

Now hang on as you "risk" this intentional encounter with the Living God!

Chapter 1
It's All About The Relationship

The following is a quote from Watchman Nee's book, <u>A Table in the Wilderness</u>, June 20. [i]

> *"There will I meet with thee, and I will commune with thee from above the mercy seat, from between the two cherubim which are upon the ark of the testimony" (Exodus 25:22).*
>
> *What is the basis of our communion with God? It is His glory. At the mercy seat with its shadowing cherubim we have fellowship with-God, and they are "cherubim of glory." It is in the place where God's glory is manifested, with its implied judgment upon man, that we find mercy there and they're alone. Cannot God, being God, show mercy where he will? No, he can only show mercy where his moral glory is also maintained. He does not divorce the mercy seat from the cherubim.*
>
> *It is the shed blood that makes communion possible for sinful man. Because of it God can show mercy without violating his glory; he can commune with man without denying himself. Thus the blood of Christ is essential to fellowship, absolutely essential. Nevertheless it is not the basis of fellowship. When I commune with blood at his mercy seat it is not on the precious blood I gaze, but on the glory. The veil is taken away, and with unveiled face we all behold the glory of God."*

As a child of God you are entitled to experience an ever-deepening relationship with the Lord. This includes enjoying fellowship in His presence, but it is much more. Matthew chapter 6 emphasizes reward in prayer as opposed to answered prayer. The reward is God Himself. Other results of prayer are simply by-products. If you are sincere about deepening your relationship with Jesus you may, but there may be a price to pay. God reveals Himself to those people who submit to and obey Him (John 14:21). God also reveals Himself to those who seek him diligently and with pure motives. Often we must remove ourselves from the familiar, and find time to set aside just for Him. God seems to honor those who hunger and thirst for true righteousness and holiness. If you do not hunger for these, at least ask God to give you that hunger.

We know that God's presence never leaves us, but I am talking about something totally different. I am talking about entering into His glory, His awesome and very private glory. This is different than corporate worship. This is just you and God in His Holy of Holies! This kind of encounter does not necessarily include a manifestation in your physical flesh. Although it may include that, it may be simply a deep inner and quiet connection. You experience His glory to such a degree that your life is eternally transformed. I am talking about a deeper baptism in the Holy Spirit, beyond the gifts. I am talking about His holiness invading you and burning off your Adamic nature. As you read on, know that when I use the word "presence" I am talking about this extra dimensional realm.

When a believer knows with faith that Jesus wants to fellowship with him, he can experience that fellowship provided he submits to God's conditions. His conditions are simply to submit to Jesus as Lord, and to quickly obey His Word. "'For all those things My hand has made, and all those things exist,' says the LORD. 'But on this one will I look *(to pay attention to)*: On him who is poor *(afflicted, humble, needy and weak)* and of a contrite spirit, and who trembles at My word'" (Isaiah 66:2). One major attribute of humility is the wiliness to repent and turn from our old ways, which are unlike God's character.

Those conditions may seem like "old stuff" for many Christians, but there is more to these than may first meet the eye. So many Christians are in "prisons" that are not necessary to be in. They have compromised being real and honest with themselves and with God. They at some point in time knew that they had compromised but now unfortunately they do not even realize that they are in "prison." Often the enemy maintains his prison doors with tactics that are very religious.

Many do not want to face pain, and refuse any type of confrontations. Therefore they compromise not receiving God's best. Others live by rules, legalism, or performance in some sort of pretended holiness. They feel that they are pleasing a harsh God. Still others live by "false grace" feeling that God understands that they are not perfect, therefore why even try to live by faith. They pray when they are in a hard place, but none of these people are enjoying the person of Jesus, the very presence and fellowship of the Creator! They may enter the Kingdom of God when they die, but they are living in Hell while they are on earth.

The Flowing River will build your faith, and will invite God to fulfill His desire to reveal Himself to you.

It will also give you some things that you need to do in order to react to His invitation. After I had known the Lord for less than one month I went to a convention and the evangelist made the statement, "The Lord is my best friend. He is closer to me than my wife." When I heard that, I became hungry for the same thing and have pursued it ever since.

Bible studies, sermons, books, discipleship lessons are all good, but if you do not experience the presence of the Lord you are missing the nugget of the Christian life. When you know that Jesus is in the room with you, everything changes. Your joy comes, afflictions seem to diminish, faith rises, and His grace becomes bigger than everything in life that you need to face.

When I discovered this Scriptural path for entering His presence called The Flowing River, my friendship and intimacy with Jesus expanded greatly. I discovered this during times when I could not sense His presence, and when things in life were not going very well with me. I discovered that I could go for a 30-minute walk and in my mind go through the Flowing

River pathway, and I would find myself at peace and in contact with the Lord. The goal is to eventually dwell in this place as a lifestyle. This is also a "what to do path" to cooperate with God for getting your practical needs supplied.

Besides enjoying God's presence, there is a very practical "what to do" path in the Flowing River.
Do we really need to follow a path?
This idea of following a pathway to enter the presence of God is in no way meant to reduce your relationship to God to a formula, or to infer that you must enter into His presence in the way I am going to describe. I do, however, believe that the Flowing River contains relationship skills that will either enhance your relationship with Jesus or perhaps even allow you to make contact for the very first time.

When my children were very young it was always up to me to initiate relationship times. However, as they grew older they began to have more choices and the relationship and fellowship that we could enjoy depended more and more on how they related to me.

The children that would come to me just for friendship, for advice, for appreciation and thanksgiving would always enter into a deeper relationship with me than if they simply came to me for an allowance or to pay a bill. I always had grace, and how they acted never varied my love for them, but I had deeper fellowship with them when they exercised their free wills and their relationship skills. Even if at times they would act in an adverse way my unconditional love would kick in (most of the time). My mercy and grace is what was supposed to draw them to me, but they needed to react and make a choice.

In a sermon recently preached at Southeastern University, Dr. Mark Rutland helped me to put some of this into proper perspective. He said the following:

> *"We are not trying to access the supernatural, but the supernatural, the Living God, Jesus Himself, is trying to access us.*

Witchcraft, sorcery, and divination attempts to contact the supernatural."

Response and obedience to God's beckoning is what gives us contact with Him in the supernatural. Again, it is God's initiative that even gives us the desire to obey Him that we might be in contact with His living presence. God is pounding at your door saying, "Please obey Me." Contact with Him often depends upon your obedience.

Obedience is a lifestyle not an event. There is a progressive ladder of obedience. As you live longer the issues for obedience grow and build upon one another. The price continually gets higher. We are called to take up our cross, and we do that. However, next time the cross carries a higher price. We never have to take up that old one again, but the new one requires more sacrifice and more obedience because the prize becomes more valuable.

Be prepared! I have seen many people experience Jesus after going through the Flowing River just one time. Make this a habit and your life will change eternally.

Chapter 2
Blessed To Be A Blessing

God's purpose is to reach a dying world and at the same time bless us. How?
We were blessed in order to become a blessing to a lost and dying world. God told our forefather Abraham, "I will bless those who bless you, and I will curse him who curses you; and in you all the families of the earth shall be blessed" (Genesis 12:3).

The only way we can bless others is to allow Jesus in us to do it through us. The only way He can do it through us is for His character to prevail over our old Adamic nature. This pathway I am going to describe is an opportunity for you to allow God to work His holiness and true righteousness into your life. As you begin to take up your cross and allow the loving God to gently chasten you, you will become more and more like Jesus, a partaker of His character. He will free you from your inner prisons, He will gently bring you to repentance about issues that are hurting you, and your life will never be the same. However, this path is not without pain. If you are lazy, if you will not confront yourself and others who are harming you, you will not enter into this life of fellowship with the Lord. As we become cleansed and become more like Jesus, we enjoy more of His presence, and our lives simply bless others.

Without holiness no man shall see God!
I thank God that righteousness and holiness are legally imputed to us as gifts. But as you deepen your relationship you begin to experience a true and actual transformation of your character into righteousness and holiness. I am not talking about some put on holiness. That kind of religious play-acting produces bitter and angry people, whereas true holiness produces joy, love, and all the fruit of the Spirit. "And that you put on the

new man which was created according to God, in true righteousness and holiness" (Ephesians 4:24).

Highway 35. The Highway of Holiness in Isaiah chapter 35.

"A highway shall be there, and a road, and it shall be called the Highway of Holiness. The unclean shall not pass over it, but it shall be for others. Whoever walks the road, although a fool, shall not go astray" (Isaiah 35:8). Isaiah chapter 33 speaks of the Israelites experiencing judgment due to their sinful lifestyle. Isaiah 34 speaks of God bringing them through the overcoming process and Isaiah chapter 35 shows the result, which is holiness. The benefits are listed in chapter 35. They include joy, singing, the desert and wastelands becoming springs of waters, deserts blooming with roses, abundant rejoicing, seeing the glory of the Lord. It describes blind eyes being opened, feebleness being healed, fear turning into faith, the thirsty given springs of water, and living above your spiritual enemies. It would do you well to study this chapter in this context.

Ezekiel 47:1-12 shows a picture of a flowing river.
The picture God showed to Ezekiel was of the Temple of God, its ordinances and design, and a river flowing from it. God spoke to Ezekiel and showed him that this was a river of life flowing from God down to the Dead Sea into the putrid waters. This river would heal the waters and make them alive. The Scripture in chapter 47 of Ezekiel says that this river started out as a small stream as it came out from under the Temple, but then it progressively became deeper and deeper until it eventually emptied into the Dead Sea. As it did, the Sea became alive with life. The sea in the Bible normally stands for the sea of lost humanity. God was showing Ezekiel that the only way that dead people could live would be to be touched by God through something called a river that was to flow from His very presence. John 7:38 says, "He who believes in Me, as the Scripture has said, out of his heart will flow rivers of living water."

The River flows in to cleanse you – The River flows out to save a dead world.

The river flows in
to cleanse us

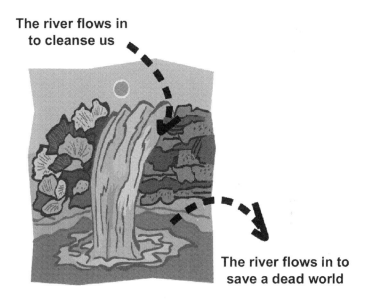

The river flows in to
save a dead world

"Write it down Ezekiel."

God told Ezekiel in chapter 43:10-11 to write down this picture of the Temple and its ordinances so that the people could see it and so that they could repent and thus be a blessing to others. That is what this Flowing River lesson is all about.

Where is the temple today? 1 Corinthians 6:19-20 says, "Or do you not know that your body is the temple of the Holy Spirit who is in you, whom you have from God, and you are not your own? For you were bought at a price; therefore glorify God in your body and in your spirit, which are God's."

We cannot become blessed nor be a blessing without the real presence of God.

We need the presence of God to set us free and cleanse us in order to do any kind of ministry, even effective prayer. Here is the pattern for experiencing the fullness of the Lord for your life, for your church and for the world. We need the presence of God to set us free and cleanse us in order to do *any* kind of ministry, even effective prayer.

Here is the pattern for experiencing the fullness of the Lord for your life.

"And they continued steadfastly in the apostles' doctrine and fellowship, in the breaking of bread, and in prayers. Then fear came upon every soul, and many wonders and signs were done through the apostles" (Acts 2:42-43).

Notice the three things the apostles did daily that resulted in many wonders and miracles:

1. The apostles' doctrine. This is the daily study of the Word of God.

2. Prayers. This most likely included more than one kind of prayer. The early church often confessed who they were in Christ, and confessed the Word.

14

3. Fellowship and breaking of bread. This was daily communion, or the taking of the cup and the bread in remembrance of the blood covenant.

The early church took communion at least weekly, if not daily. It was their way to enter into the presence of God and experience a deep knowing of Him in a personal way. It was not a religious practice, it was a time of enjoying Him in a real way.

The purpose of communion was to bring the partakers into God's presence. Read Luke 24:30-31 as an example. In it they found healing and all their needs supplied. The presence of God, through His flesh and blood covenant, meets all our needs. (Taken from Dick Reuben's video series, "A Pattern for Revival Fire: Covenant Meal - The Lord's Table.")

The Flowing River is a daily exercise that does the same thing (not to replace communion, but in addition to it). The Flowing River walks one through the blood covenant and brings the person through the veil, which is His flesh, into the Holy of Holies right into His presence! We need His presence daily, not just once in a while!

In John 6:51 Jesus says that He is the Living Bread that came down from Heaven. Hebrews 10:19-20 talks about a new and living way of coming into the Holy of Holies through the veil that is the flesh of Jesus.

What all of this is saying is that the way into the presence of God is through the recognition of the blood covenant; His blood and flesh. You will see that going through the Flowing River recognizes the blood covenant much in the same way as does communion.

We need to know that there are enemies that want to stop God from being real to us.
Our enemies come at us in three main ways:
Our will -
Our mind -
Our emotions -
Are all attacked by Our Flesh, the World and Satan.

Question:
How do we overcome these enemies to get into God's presence for fellowship?

Answer:
God has already provided for all victory over all enemies! The way into His presence was provided at the Cross when the veil was torn from top to bottom - Mark 15:38. Now it is our job to cooperate. We must take up our cross - that will give us the victory!

Luke 9:23-25 (KJV) says, "And he said to them all, 'If any man will come after me, let him deny himself, and take up his cross daily, and follow me. For whosoever will save his life shall lose it: but whosoever will lose his life for my sake, the same shall save it. For what is a man advantaged, if he gain the whole world, and lose himself, or be cast away?'"

The word for *life* in Luke 9 means "*soul*" or the will, mind and emotions. The word *deny* means to say *no* to.

The key to abundant life and receiving all that Jesus has for us, including His presence, is to complete the blood covenant by taking up our cross.

Many of us know the magnificent, all inclusive, all powerful work done by Jesus on the Cross of Calvary; how He shed his blood for our sin, and rose from the dead to give us life. We cannot add to that. However, in order to take advantage of that work, we must also die. We must take up our cross, deny ourselves and follow Him. We must lose our life.

Our relationship and fellowship with God are based upon a blood covenant. To the Western mindset that can be a foreign thing. The closest comparison we have is marriage, and so many people have an understanding of this relationship that is contrary to the Bible. Ask yourself this: Would you negotiate with your mate-to-be on how many other intimate relationships you are allowed after your marriage?

Two deaths, Jesus' and yours, activate the blood covenant!

16

What is so important about a blood covenant?

1 Peter 1:18-19 says, "knowing that you were not redeemed with corruptible things, like silver or gold, from your aimless conduct received by tradition from your fathers, but with the precious blood of Christ, as of a lamb without blemish and without spot."

Leviticus 17:11 says, "For the life of the flesh is in the blood, and I have given it to you upon the altar to make atonement for your souls; for it is the blood that makes atonement for the soul."

The spiritual life can be exchanged by the law of substitution. A blood covenant changes your family inheritance.

Family inheritance.

This basically means that people may be born into a certain family, and from that family lineage they will receive blessings and curses as their inheritance. However, blessings and curses can be changed. Tribes in Africa, in American Indian culture and some Asian type societies have always looked for ways to swap or trade blessings and curses with other people.

Since ancient times, people have drank blood that was offered to their god, so that they could be like God.

Before the Foundation of the World, God prearranged to have Jesus crucified according to the *eternal* Spirit, which means that the substitution principle was in effect before any man was created (Revelation 13:8).

In order for a blood covenant to truly be effective, there must be blood shed by two parties, or there must be two deaths and two crosses. We must die to our self and commit all we are and all we have to Jesus. The good thing is that Jesus also commits all He has and all He is to us!

When we connect the Cross of Jesus to our cross we are plugged into God, and power happens! There are always two crosses that must connect to make a blood covenant.

Chapter 3
The Tabernacle

The Tabernacle is a powerful symbol of the two crosses to use as a prayer guide.
It will help us take up our cross and walk us into the very presence of God for FELLOWSHIP!

The following is a quote from <u>God's Plan and the Overcomers</u> by Watchman Nee [ii].

> *The Old Testament tells us how the chosen people of God lived on earth. At first, the tabernacle served as the center of the 12 tribes; later it was the temple that became their center. The center of the temple was the ark. The tabernacle, the temple and the ark are all types of Christ. As long as the children of Israel maintained their proper relationship with the tabernacle or the temple they were victorious, and no nation could overcome them. Even though their enemies learned how to fight while they themselves were not familiar with fighting, the children of Israel overcame all their enemies nonetheless. But the moment they had problems with the tabernacle or the temple, they were taken into captivity. Nothing else, whether they had powerful kings or great wisdom in themselves mattered at all; the only concern, which mattered, was whether or not they had offended the ark of the tabernacle or temple. If the Lord had the preeminence, then theirs was the victory. So too with us today. In minding the victory of Christ, we also have the victory.*

As you journey into fellowship with God, picture taking a walk through the Tabernacle as the priests of the Old Testament did.

God's reason for the Tabernacle was to apply blood in order to restore the Glory of intimate fellowship.

The Tabernacle

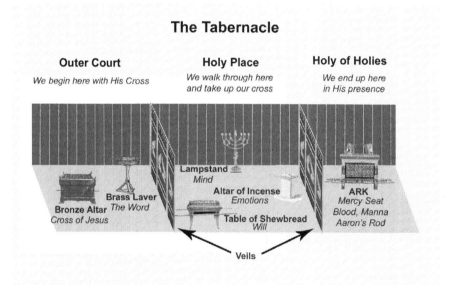

Outer Court	Holy Place	Holy of Holies
We begin here with His Cross	*We walk through here and take up our cross*	*We end up here in His presence*

Lampstand
Mind

Altar of Incense
Emotions

Brass Laver
Bronze Altar *The Word*
Cross of Jesus

Table of Shewbread
Will

ARK
Mercy Seat
Blood, Manna
Aaron's Rod

Veils

Why is the Tabernacle such an important symbol in restoring intimacy with God

Notice in chart 1 that God and Adam enjoyed fellowship and intimacy before sin entered.

Notice in chart 2, that after sin entered, the Glory of fellowship was broken. "For all have sinned and fall short of the glory of God." (Romans 3:23)

It required blood to bridge the broken fellowship, forgiveness of our sin. This is the value of forgiveness.

The two courts, the Outer Court and the Holy Place represent His Cross and our cross, the blood of both parties.

"There will I meet thee, and i will commune with thee from above and mercy seat, from between the two cherubin which are upon the ark of the testimony." (Exodus 25:22)

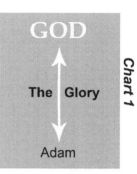

The Glory

Adam

The Glory Patter after the sin.
All fall short of the Glory of God

The Glory broken

Adam

Chart 1

Chart 2

The Tabernacle added two chambers to restore the Glory through the blood.

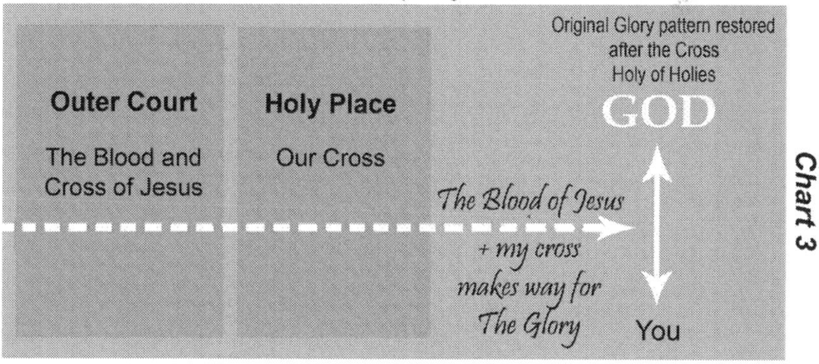

Original Glory pattern restored after the Cross
Holy of Holies

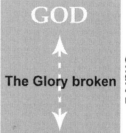

Outer Court

The Blood and Cross of Jesus

Holy Place

Our Cross

The Blood of Jesus + my cross makes way for The Glory

You

Chart 3

There are two crosses in a blood covenant.

First: His Cross
Under the Old Covenant, Israel held an annual day of atonement, called Yom Kippur. The sins of Israel were to be dealt with on this one day of the year when the high priest prepared to go through the Tabernacle on behalf of Israel for their sins.

At the Bronze Altar, in the outer court, there were two young goats, called calves. One was given a scarlet cloth around its neck indicating it would be slain for blood. The other was tied up outside the gate indicating it was to be the scapegoat. The first goat was slain at the altar and the priest took its blood into the Holy of Holies, where he presented it with incense off the altar of incense (the place of praise). As the incense burned, it filled the Holy of Holies with smoke, which represented (and actually, released) the presence of God. The priest would sprinkle the blood on the mercy seat once and in front of it seven times. Outside, every person in the camp lay prostrate through all of this. No one saw any of it happening, yet it meant that his or her sins would be forgiven for the entire year.

Next, as the priest returned and changed his clothes, he laid his hands on the head of the other goat, the scapegoat, symbolizing the transfer of all of the sins to the head of the animal. There was to be a very rugged man chosen to take the scapegoat into the desert wilderness and lead it to a place where it could not return. He would take it to an inescapable place. They would go to a valley surrounded by ledges and cliffs and the goat was lowered down so it could never escape (Leviticus 16:21-22).

Now as the priest laid hands on the scapegoat, beginning the second part of the ceremony, he confessed the sins of the entire Israel. He would say, "Lord, place my sins and the sins of the people on the head of this goat. Now go and depart." As they led the goat out of the camp, all of the people stood and rejoiced. They could all see and understand, even the children. The scapegoat is symbolic of Jesus being our scapegoat, being lowered into Hell for us with our sins on His head. He took our sin and removed it forever, never again to be found or to return. Psalm 103:12 says, "As far as the east is from the west, so far has He removed our transgressions from us." Micah 7:19b (KJV) says, "and thou wilt cast all their sins into the depths of the sea."

Hebrews 9:12-14 (KJV) says, "Neither by the blood of goats and calves, but by his own blood he entered in once into the holy place, having obtained eternal redemption for us. For if the blood of bulls and of goats, and the ashes of an heifer sprinkling the unclean, sanctifieth to the purifying of the flesh: How much more shall the blood of Christ, who through the eternal Spirit offered himself without spot to God, purge your conscience from dead works to serve the living God?"

Second: Our Cross

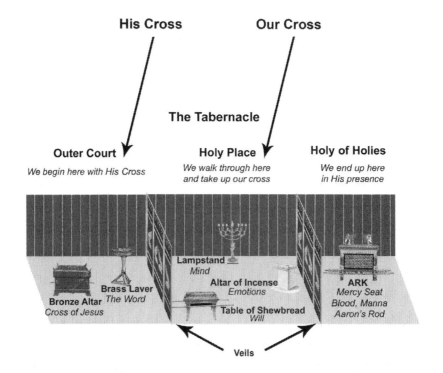

His Cross

Our Cross

The Tabernacle

Outer Court

We begin here with His Cross

Holy Place

We walk through here and take up our cross

Holy of Holies

We end up here in His presence

Lampstand
Mind

Brass Laver
Bronze Altar *The Word*
Cross of Jesus

Altar of Incense
Emotions

Table of Shewbread
Will

ARK
Mercy Seat
Blood, Manna
Aaron's Rod

Veils

When Jesus said that we must deny ourselves, lose our life for His sake, etc., He was using a word that refers to our soul. So we must deny, or say *no* to our soul.

Our soul has three parts: will, mind (intellect), and emotions. The Holy Place represents that part of our being, the soul. It has three pieces of furniture that represent our Will, Mind, and Emotions (see above picture). Saying *no* to these and *yes* to what God has is the taking up of our cross.

Our will -
Our mind -
Our emotions-
are attacked by Our Flesh, the World and Satan.

What is taking up your cross all about?

We teach here in this Flowing River chapter that we need to "take up our cross" in order to realize the Glory of God, His presence in our own personal lives.

In the Garden of Eden Eve thought that she could have both the Glory of God and independence. She did not believe that taking the path to independence, the Tree of Knowledge of Good and Evil, would lead to such a tragic end. In doing so she would not only lose the Glory of God in her life, but she would enter a realm that she had never agreed to specifically. That realm is what the Bible calls the world system, the Whore of Babylon, the evil woman as described in Proverbs 7.

God told her if she ate of her own independence that she would die, or literally, be separated from God. She did not realize what that really meant.

She had not experienced the dead end of the world's way. She thought God had lied, and that gave her insecurity.

"But I fear, lest somehow, as the serpent deceived Eve by his craftiness, so your minds may be corrupted from the simplicity that is in Christ" (2 Corinthians 11:3).

Eve had the total Glory of God and yet was tempted away. That shows that the temptation, the lie, is very strong for you and for me. Often it takes our experiencing the failure of the World's way in order to value Jesus just for Who He is, and do whatever is needed to prepare for His Glory in our lives.

We need to understand that our independence by default takes us to the Whore, the world. There is no other choice except for God. We are deceived because we don't know that independence takes us right into the arms of the Harlot.

The Harlot is spoken about in Proverbs 7. It shows how the World, the Harlot, entices people. Then compare that to Proverbs 8, which talks about Wisdom, which is Jesus Himself and how He lures people.

When I saw Jesus in 1979 I already knew that there was nothing in the way of the World that was of any value. I saw that nothing in the World's system works. I was in bondage to it and controlled by it.

Taking up our cross really means agreeing to God's ways, especially if they are painful and not comfortable at the time, but knowing that it will lead to our benefit, our abundant life and to God's eternal purpose for us and His Kingdom.

We cannot take up our cross without help?

We can only take up our cross to a point, but not all the way. We don't have enough hands to crucify all of ourselves; the last nail must be inserted by the world. We must experience some sort of pain and breaking to really get the job done. God does not do this, the world does. We can offer to God those things that we control, those things that we are aware of. However, God sees with vision we do not have. He knows those things in your soul that are keeping you from complete healing and connection with Him. The more of you that can die, the more of Him can live in you. His plan is not to clean up your old life, but to have you experience the crucifixion with Him.

Now we will take a journey to each of these items in our prayer time and journey right past our enemies into the very presence of God!

Chapter 4
Daily Prayer Guide

"The Flowing River"
(Daily Prayer Guide)

To Journey Into
The Presence of God

Instructions:

1. First, read the first three chapters, then re-read them again at least once a month. Then, start here on this page on a daily basis, taking at least twenty minutes to make contact with God.

2. When you start through the tabernacle your back is to be toward the world and your face toward Jesus. This is important, for the Holy Spirit will not honor you with His presence if you are facing in the wrong direction (spiritual direction, Acts 26:18).

3. Go to each "stop" and deal with that subject in prayer with the Lord. Look up some of the Scriptures. Be alert for areas of repentance, for this is one of our main contributions toward this fellowship time with God.

4. It is preferred that you go through all these stops at one time. You can do it in *twenty minutes*. However, if you do not have time in one sitting to go through this entire process, do not give up. Instead, begin the process in the morning, and go through at least one step. Then, do the next one at lunch. If you need to, go ahead and continue the next day. Eventually, live a life of this process and it will be a natural process of always staying in His presence.

Relationship Disciplines and Skills.

Here are some relationship disciplines that we feel are extremely important if you are going to pursue an authentic relationship with the Lord Jesus.

God is inviting you to discipline your life to relate to Him and get to know Him. This is how the blood covenant blessings flow into your life:

1. Make a firm decision to pursue the relationship. Offer yourself completely to God (Romans 12:1-2). This is our blood covenant response to a mighty blood covenant offered to us by God.

2. Take time to listen. You must take in His Word. Words are blood covenant containers. You must always be in a disciplined Bible study of some kind. Ask the Holy Spirit to show you.

3. Take time to talk. Speak your words. Some people write down your thoughts and feelings in a journal, which can be very valuable. If you have never taken time to be honest with God, you should write down your thoughts, emotions and feelings daily in a journal. You will see God speak back to you! Be gut-level honest. Honesty with your blood covenant partner Jesus will cause your sin to go on Him. You cannot and will not overcome any bondage without this gut level honesty.

4. Take time to talk. Speak His Words. Read Psalms and Proverbs by the day. One discipline is to read aloud five Psalms every morning. Use the system of the calendar. As an example, on the 24th of the month read Psalms 24, 54, 84, 114 and 144. Also read Proverbs 24. In this system the student will read all Psalms and Proverbs every month. Using this system renews the mind, speaks the Word to Satan, and allows the suffering believer to relate his/her emotions to the Psalmist's. Provisions can be made for months with 31 days, and for Psalm 119. God may lead you to other Scriptures to read out loud as you progress, but this is a good start, and can be a continued blessing for the rest of your life.

5. Obey God. Ask God to give you something simple, something small every day that you may obey. It may be just encouraging another. It may be not driving down the same street that fed your addiction. It may be confessing your sin to Him.

This is a big thing!

John 14:21-23 says that when we obey His Word that He will reveal more and more of Himself to us. Once you have "seen" Jesus, your relationship with Him will no longer be a discipline, but it will be a passionate pursuit. The apostle Paul had this passion when he said in Philippians 3:10 (Amplified Bible), "[For my determined purpose is] that I may know Him [that I may progressively become more deeply and intimately acquainted with Him, perceiving and recognizing and understanding the wonders of His Person more strongly and more clearly], and that I may in that same way come to know the power outflowing from His resurrection [which it exerts over believers], and that I may so share His sufferings as to be continually transformed [in spirit into His likeness even] to His death, [in the hope]."

6. Communion. Take communion on a regular basis. Many people take it daily.

7. Stay in fellowship. It is important to be in fellowship with strong Bible-believing, Spirit-filled believers, for refreshing and encouragement.

You need to walk in love, and when you fail, run to God to be cleansed.

"For the law of the Spirit of life in Christ Jesus has made me free from the law of sin and death" (Romans 8:2). If we stay turned toward God and stay honest with Him, He will see us through even in our mistakes and stumbling.

Look at the Flowing River Appendix A and give yourself an honest evaluation. If there are no known sins, then confess Galatians 2:20 and 2 Corinthians 5:21.

Now walk with me through the Tabernacle into the Holy of Holies.

The Outer Court

First Stop: The Bronze Altar – The Cross of Jesus.

Brazen Altar

Forgiveness.
The blood covenant swaps everything that we have that is bad for everything that God has that is good. However, we cannot have forgiveness of sins without making Jesus Lord (Romans 10:9-10).

Start out today by being honest with Jesus. 1 John 1:9 says, "If we confess our sins, He is faithful and just to forgive us our sins and cleanse us from all unrighteousness."

A big part of taking up your cross is being GUT-LEVEL HONEST with God. You need to be totally transparent and tell Him everything. Take time to pour out your heart to him as you would your best friend! 1 John 1:7 says, "But if we walk in the light as He is in the light, we have fellowship with one another, and the blood of Jesus Christ His Son cleanses us from all sin." Jesus said in John 3:19 that sin had no power as long as people came out into the light with the truth, and did not attempt to hide in darkness. Jesus did not die for our excuses; He died for our sin!

Following is a Spiritual Check-up, a list of issues for which we all might need forgiveness.

Appendix A
A Spiritual Check-up.

- Love – Are you treating others with the unconditional love of God?
- Selfishness – Putting your own needs over the needs of others. Love is concerned with the welfare of the other person; are you more concerned with yourself and how you feel?
- Stealing – Can you remember taking money for property that was not yours?
- Cheating – Did you get anything from anyone unfairly?
- Lying – Any designed form of deception.
- Slander – Speaking evil of someone. You do not have to lie to slander. Have you spoken about others without love?
- Immorality – Are you guilty of stirring up desires that you could not righteously feed? Sexual vice, all impurity, even against your own body.
- Drunkenness, drugs sorcery, carousing.
- Foul or polluted language, evil words, unwholesome or worthless talk. Filthiness, foolish, silly, and corrupt talk.
- Envy – Behind the talk of other's failures and faults usually lurks envy.
- Ingratitude – How many times have others done things for you that you are not grateful for?
- Anger – Have you been bad-tempered?
- Cursing – Have you used gutter language?
- Needless silly talk. Talking and acting like a moron. Jests and practical jokes that tend to undermine the sacred and precious standards of life. Have you made fun of an ethnic group or a certain part of the world, a state or region in your country, or some politician? Ethnic and regional jokes have no place in holiness.

- Hardness – Did you fight back, murmur or return evil for evil?
- Habits – Have you continually over-indulged natural appetites; how about your eating habits?
- Half-heartedness – Can you remember times when you deliberately shirked your full share of responsibility?
- Hindrance – Have you destroyed another's confidence in you by needlessly taking up their time? Have you betrayed another's confidence in you?
- Hypocrisy – Did the life you lived before some people make all you said of Christ and His gospel a lie?
- Broken Vows – Is there a vow you made to God that you have not kept?
- Unforgiveness – Are you holding any resentment against anyone, friend or foe?
- Divisions, clicks, the party spirit of having differing groups.
- Lustful, rich and wasteful living, greediness. Overspending on shopping, Wasting time.
- Not treating wives, husbands, children, and parents with love and honor.
- Not being content, being jealous of what others have and you do not have.
- Love of money – A person without any money can still have the love of money.
- Idolatry – Any desire in your life above your desire for God.
- Strife – Have you stirred up strife by unneeded words?
- Witchcraft – Manipulating another to meet your needs.
- Rebellion to authority – Boss, teacher, parent, spiritual leader, etc.
- Love of the World – Includes: Sins of the eyes - What are you reading or watching? Lust of the flesh - What are you desiring? Pride of life - What part of your life do you think you can handle without God being involved? - Pretending in thought or life to be more or less than you really ARE.
- Pride is the greatest sin of all. Examine these areas:
- Do you focus on the failure of others or are you concerned with your own sense of spiritual need?

- Are you self-righteous and critical or compassionate and forgiving, looking for the best in others?
- Do you look down on others or esteem all others better than yourself?
- Are you independent and self-sufficient or dependent, recognizing your need for others?
- Must you maintain control or do you surrender control?
- Do you have to prove you are correct, or are you willing to yield the right to be correct?
- Do you have a demanding spirit or a giving spirit?
- Do you desire to be served or are you motivated to serve others?
- Do you desire to be promoted or are you happy when others are promoted?
- Do you need to receive the credit or are you happy when others are recognized?
- Do you feel confident in how much you know or are you humbled by how much you have yet to learn?
- Are you self-conscious or not concerned with yourself at all?
- Do you keep people at arm's length or do you risk getting close to others. Are you willing to take the risk of loving intimately?
- Are you quick to blame others or do you accept responsibility?
- Are you unapproachable or easy to be entreated?
- Are you defensive when criticized or receive criticism with a humble and open heart?
- Are you concerned with being respected or being real?
- Are you concerned about what others think or what God thinks?
- Do you work to maintain your image or do you die to your reputation?
- Do you find it difficult to share your spiritual needs with others or are you willing to be open and transparent?
- Do you try to hide your sin or are you willing to be exposed when you are wrong?

- Do you have a hard time saying, "I was wrong, will you please forgive me?"
- When confessing sin, do you deal in generalities or do you deal in specifics?
- Are you remorseful over your sin when you get caught or are you grieved over your sin and quick to repent?
- When there is a misunderstanding or conflict, do you wait for others to come and ask forgiveness or do you take the initiative?
- Do you compare yourself with others and feel deserving of honor or do you compare yourself to the holiness of God and feel a desperate need for mercy?
- Do you think you have little or nothing to repent for or do you have a continual attitude of repentance.
- Do you think that everyone else needs revival or do you continually sense a need for a fresh encounter with the filling of the Holy Spirit?
- Are you proud when you are around a new Christian or do you delight in his/her zeal? Are you willing to learn from him/her?
- Are you intimidated when you are around a more mature Christian, or are you hungry to learn from his/her experience?

Surgery needed?

If the Holy Spirit shows us sin, we must go back to the place where the Lord first met us. It is the Cross again. We see the Lord Jesus once crucified for that sin, bearing our penalty.

A line of blood trickles down from the Cross' splintered base. The sight should shock and grieve us because we see the awfulness of God's judgment. We need to understand that all of God's wrath and judgment was put on Jesus at the Cross.

Jesus is waiting there for us, not to condemn us, but happy to have us come to the Cross to give Him our sin. So many Christians run from God in shame and guilt when they discover sin. Past sins, mistakes and bad decisions, if left unchecked, will block God's presence from you.

God wants you to grow up and learn and not make the same mistakes again, however, bringing you into His presence without shame and guilt is extremely important to Him. That is the only way you can glorify God and be free from all bondages. Romans 8:1-2 says that there is indeed the Law of sin and death. What you sow is what you will reap. The law of sowing and reaping is absolute for the good seed, however, for the bad seed there is a remedy. That remedy is the Law of the Spirit of life, which nullifies the Law of sin and death.

"There is therefore now no condemnation to those who are in Christ Jesus, who do not walk according to the flesh, but according to the Spirit. For the law of the Spirit of life in Christ Jesus has made me free from the law of sin and death. For what the law could not do in that it was weak through the flesh, God did by sending His own Son in the likeness of sinful flesh, on account of sin: He condemned sin in the flesh, that the righteous requirement of the law might be fulfilled in us who do not walk according to the flesh but according to the Spirit" (Romans 8:1-4).

God's remedy for sin is to come to the Cross, come to the Holy of Holies into His presence and let His character flood your character. His holiness will replace your sin. This is the only remedy. We cannot do it ourselves. It is the displacement method. We do not empty out our sin, God floods us with His holiness and love and the sin must leave. Do not be discouraged if you have to do this time and time again. God is not the one who condemns, Satan is. God will take you back as many times as you come. When you stop coming is when He is grieved.

Walk out into the light of reality. Drop your self-deceit and face this sin for what it really is. Turn from it, from your heart. Take sides with God against it. Purpose in your heart NEVER to go back into that sin again.

Confession:
"If we confess our sins, He is faithful and just to forgive us our sins and to cleanse us from all unrighteousness" (1 John 1:9).

"The LORD is merciful and gracious, slow to anger, and abounding in mercy. He will not always strive with us, nor will He keep His anger forever. He has not dealt with us according to our sins, nor punished us according to our iniquities. For as the heavens are high above the earth, so great is His mercy toward those who fear Him; as far as the east is from the west, so far has He removed our transgressions from us" (Psalm 103:8-12).

Forgiveness is not the same as excusing.

Forgiveness is a strong word that means to cut away and remove like a surgeon cuts out a cancer. Forgiveness of sin means that the sin is removed from you and put on to Jesus who bore it on the Cross. We do not excuse a wrong done to us. That would not be right. However, we do forgive it, we take it off of the person and put it on Jesus.

Confession is agreeing with how God sees the matter and speaking it with your mouth. Confession is not just saying it, confession includes being in agreement with the Word. Humility is admitting you are wrong.

Will you do this now? Will you go to your gracious and loving Father as a little child and humbly ask His forgiveness and confess your sin?

"Oh God, You know my foolishness, and my sin is not hid from You... for Your Name's sake, pardon my iniquity, for it is great... If you, Lord, would mark iniquities, who shall stand? But there is forgiveness with You, that You may be feared.

Oh God, my Father, I come to you to confess my sin(s) of: (Now list and confess them.)

Your Word says that these acts and/or these attitudes are sin, and I hereby agree with Your Word. I call this sin what it is. I make no excuses for it. I no longer want to hold this sin in my spirit, soul and body. I want to get it out and expel it. It is separating me from You. It is destroying me. I want to be healed, spirit, soul and body, and I want to be close to you. I accept your forgiveness. Thank you for putting this sin on Jesus, and thank you that He took it to His Cross for me. I know I do not deserve this exchange, but I am so thankful to be free."

Restitution is the willingness to pay back or restore wherever possible. If you are now forgiven before the Lord, are you ready to ask Him for the courage to confess and restore to others you have wronged? Your conscience must be clean before both God AND man if you want to know true freedom. You cannot stand for God with a dirty past in other's eyes.

Memories of your failure in their eyes will drive you deeper into bondage each time you remember them. If you have not asked their forgiveness, your guilt will kill your faith and rob you of direction and purpose. You will not, of course, have to confess every sin to everyone; just the sins committed against the ones you know you have wronged.

The rule: The circle of confession should only go as far as the circle of committal. Those sins against God alone, you have left with His loving forgetfulness (Psalm 103:8-13; Isaiah 43:25; Jeremiah 31:34). Those against God and man must be made right with BOTH God and the person(s) wronged.

Portions of this Appendix A were taken from Winkie Pratney's tracts published on the World Wide Web, used by permission.

Second Stop: The Laver – The Word of God.

Brass Laver

Now that our conscience is clear and we can make contact with God, let's get into the Word.

The Word says that the priest would die if he tried to get into the Holy Place without stopping at the Laver. We cannot proceed into God's presence without being cleansed by the Word of God (Ephesians 5:26-27).

The Laver will cleanse us from the filth of the world. It will also be a mirror to judge us; it will bring things to our mind that we need to get right with God. The Word will renew our mind so that we can think spiritually and stand against the words that demons speak into our minds.

The Word also tells us that Satan is judged (John 16:11). Be sure to say this out loud, "Satan you have been judged a loser!"

Spend an abundant amount of time in the Word!

    a. Use your devotional book.

    b. Use your ISOB or other Bible study book.

    c. Read the Proverb for today.

    d. Read one or more Psalms.

    e. Read other books about the Bible, or just read the Bible and ask the Holy Spirit to interpret. Read through the Bible in a year's time.

    f. Listen to some teaching or music tapes that have the Word.

Third Stop: The First Veil – Thanksgiving.

First Veil: Thanksgiving

Come into His gates with Thanksgiving, into His courts with Praise. Now that you have been in the Word, you know you are right with God, Satan is judged. You have a lot to be thankful for! Even if you do not have things around you to be thankful for, try to find some. Thank Him that you are saved and going to Heaven.

Just thank Him for what the Word says. Thank Him because the Word says to and because you know you have victory if you hang on. Thank Him for the promises that He made to you that have not come into your life as yet. Thank Him because you know that He wants to take all of unfavorable circumstances in your life and turn them into something beautiful. Thanking Him is a major relationship skill. Children always stay in better relationship with their parents when they are grateful as opposed to always begging and complaining.

We need to remember Colossians 1:20, which says, "and by Him to reconcile all things to Himself, by Him, whether things on earth or things in heaven, having made peace through the blood of His cross." We can thank Him because no matter how difficult the suffering or challenge is in our lives, this verse promises that everything can be reconciled, or turned into a friend through His blood of the cross. Was His crucifixion turned into a friend? Yes! Then your challenges can be also.

Now you are entering the Holy Place.

Fourth Stop: The Table of Shewbread – Your Will.

Table of Shewbread

The next Stop is inside the Holy Place. This is where you give Jesus your will for His will, your mind for His mind, your emotions for His emotions. This is taking up your cross, denying yourself and following Jesus (Luke 9:23). Only you can tell God to take all of your heart, He will not violate your will. He needs to hear you tell Him about the things of your will that you are surrendering to Him.

Exchange the desires of your heart (even if they may be good) for God's plan or will for your life. Lay down your wants, desires and plans and ask God for His.

God is continually looking at our will; that is what Shewbread means. Bread is ground up flour, mixed with oil and baked in the fire. Our will and our desires must be continually offered up to the altar to be ground and burned. This is a very special sacrifice to God, for it is *our* will, and He will not overwhelm, nor control us. Offer your body a living sacrifice, so that we may prove that perfect will of God (Romans 12:1-2).

Make up your mind to forgive even if you do not feel like it.

This is an opportunity to repent, to turn from the paths and ways of the world toward God's paths. When we turn, we get the power of God (Acts 26:18; 2 Corinthians 3:16).

Exchange the lusts of the flesh for the fruit of the Spirit. The fruit of the Spirit: love, joy, peace, patience, kindness, goodness, faithfulness, gentleness and self-control (Galatians 5:19-23).

Fifth Stop: The Golden Lampstand – Your mind.

Golden Lampstand

Exchange your old thoughts for the mind of Christ. 2 Corinthians 10:4-6 tells us the warfare is in our mind. It tells us that strongholds are our reasonings that holds captive our thoughts, and these thoughts keep us from the true knowledge of God. There is much to be said here because our thoughts are the very core of our being. We must set our thoughts free! How? When we were slaves to sin, we used the Tree of Knowledge of Good and Evil, which is our reasoning. Now we should be using the Tree of Life, which is the Word of God. I no longer think and decide, but I use my mind for it's God given purpose, and that is to listen and obey! This alone will destroy the strongholds in our minds. When we truly see the Glory of God as Paul did on the road to Damascus, we no longer reason, we simply say, "Lord, what do you desire for me to do?" Take your negative thoughts captive by bringing them honestly to the Cross; giving them to Jesus as something you do not want. This is powerful!

Demons constantly accuse us and bombard our minds with half-truths. Isaiah 11 tells us that God replaces our natural intellect with that of the Holy Spirit: i.e., Spirit of the Lord, knowledge, counsel, wisdom, understanding, might and fear of the Lord.

Take your thoughts captive as in 2 Corinthians 10:4-6.

Airports now have security checkpoints that screen each person and each piece of luggage for dangerous items before boarding an airplane. You do the same thing. When you sense a thought, stop, and ask, "Does this thought carry dangerous consequences? Is this thought profitable for me to live a godly life? Is this thought from Satan, or my flesh?" At that point, you simply make a decision to say to that thought, "I do not allow you entrance. Access denied. I take you captive and evict you in the name of Jesus. I order you to come into obedience to Christ the Word and go into death."

After some practice you will better recognize those thoughts that come from God. Often God's thoughts come as spontaneous thoughts. Sometimes to me they feel like a bolt of lighting that just zooms through your spirit.

Replace your thoughts with godly thoughts.

You cannot just leave a vacuum; you must fill your mind with something good.

We need to get our mind renewed by the Holy Spirit and the Word of God (Romans 12:2). Sometimes our intellect does not know how to pray. Romans 8:26 says that we should use our prayer language to pray God's perfect will. Every time you use your prayer language, you are praying out God's Word and God's will. Your speech center dominates the entire brain, so your mind is being renewed and smoothed out to tell your flesh to conform to God's will.

The Helmet of Salvation.

Our brain needs salvation from cleverness, from allowing our mind and intellect to take God's place in our lives. Without this, we will never walk in God's perfect will for our lives (Romans 12:1-2). More often than not, this is not something that we can or will voluntarily give up. Usually it takes a "breaking," a set of circumstances that take us beyond what our brain can negotiate and/or solve. Only then can we quietly wait on God for Him to speak and be silent while He works out our lives.

The Lampstand traditionally represents testimony. We should utilize our intellectual powers to speak God's Word as a testimony to the enemy.

Sixth Stop: The Altar of Incense – Your Emotions.

Altar of Incense

Exchange your old emotions induced by your flesh and the World for God's fruit of peace, joy, love, hope, etc. It is interesting that after we have given God our will and our thinking, then we can trust our emotions. Emotions should not drive us, but should be the result and by-product of a will and mind that has been consecrated to God.

This is the place of a sacrifice of praise. Read Psalms 145-150 out loud if you do not *feel* the praise in your heart. God is seeking those who worship Him in Spirit and in Truth (John 4:24). From this point of praise, God will seek you and desire your company!

Give Him those emotions that you have been holding back; perhaps your tears, maybe the raising of your hands, or perhaps just revealing to Him your true emotions. Go ahead, no one is looking except Him! Leave your past hurts, discouragements, depression and lack of emotional expression behind and just praise Him. His life will take over and you will know He lives in you!

In front of this altar is the thick veil that hides the Holy of Holies and the presence of God. God wants you to come through the veil more than you desire to. He will pull you through. No natural man could go here without dying.

This veil tore from top to bottom when Jesus died on the Cross, giving us entry into God's presence by His blood and indicating that His death removed the obstacle that sin created for coming into the very presence of God. Praise Him for this fact.

Chapter 5
Inside The Holy of Holies

The Holy of Holies is the place where there is no light except for God. The High Priest could only go here once a year, and only under certain conditions. The incense censor from this altar actually went into the Holy of Holies with the High Priest once a year. This symbolizes that your praise and worship do not stop here but that they are the entry into His presence, and they go with us.

Your Spirit: The Ark of the Covenant – God's presence.

Ark of the Covenant

Your destination. Now God pulls you through the veil into the Holy of Holies – the very presence of God.

Here is the Ark of the Covenant. It is covered by the Mercy Seat that is sprinkled with blood. We needed mercy at the Bronze Altar, the Cross, in the very beginning. However, now in His presence is a new dimension of realizing His mercy and the blood of Jesus in a way that only the Holy Spirit can show you. His mercy endures forever. It is almost impossible to write about, it must be experienced. This is when the seed of the Word is planting in your heart. When the Word of God is anointed by the presence of the Holy Spirit, it is powerful!

On either side are huge angels protecting everything. There is no light in here at all except for the Light of God.

Remember, the Ark of the Covenant is now in our heart! It is no longer an external thing. We are the Temple of God. Meditate on that. "Do you not know that you are the temple of God and that the Spirit of God dwells in you?" (1 Corinthians 3:16).

The Ark contents symbolize three main things:
Tablets of Law:
This is a precious reminder that the Law of God is written on our hearts. It is no longer a list of do's and don'ts. We are saved by His life, not His death. His death cleansed us so that His life could inhabit us.

The law in our hearts represent godly character, the fruit of the Spirit. This is ours.

The manna, or the Word of God:
When you are in God's presence, the revealed Word of God comes alive! The Bible becomes Scriptures, the Scriptures become the Word, and the Word becomes flesh. The Word is now in you! If you have time, this is a great place to open your Bible and let the Lord speak.

Manna also speaks of our provisions. All of our provisions, love, security and significance are already inside of us. This includes everything we need for life and godliness. Fruit for our provisions here on earth is provided by God's Word (2 Peter 1:1-11).

We are eligible to bear "manna fruit." That is provisions provided by the supernatural Word of God, rather than our own efforts and plans.

Aaron's Rod:
This signifies our anointed ministry to be workers and prayer warriors for God. There were 12 broken almond rods placed in the Temple at God's command. The one that would supernaturally bud during the night, would be the one whose owner would be God's appointed minister. Only God has our ministry for us, and we only realize what it is when we are in His presence (Numbers 17:8).

When we bear the fruit of Aaron's Rod, our ministry and outreach just happens supernaturally, rather then by our human efforts and plans.

Here is where we can really receive the promises of God in His Word. When we receive them here, we know that we will have them! Philippians 4:19 says, "And my God shall supply all your need according to His riches in glory by Christ Jesus." Here you are in Glory! Here are all the riches of Heaven waiting for you.

Begin to thank God that these three things are not just in front of you, but they are *in* you. Not only are they *in* you, but also the blood and mercy seat and angels are protecting you with them. Psalm 91 says that the angels protect you in your way of service and obedience.

Now you are equipped to be a real intercessor. You are sharing in the High Priestly ministry of Jesus and praying for others effectively. Jesus said in John 15:7, "If you abide in Me, and My words abide in you, you will ask what you desire, and it shall be done for you."

Taking up your cross brings fruit.
God's presence for fellowship is not the only reason for taking up your cross to come into the Holy of Holies, but it accomplishes another very powerful thing.

It activates God's fruit within you for supernatural activities in your life and in your realm of influence. Notice, in the Ark, the three potential items of fruit: fruit of character, fruit for provisions, and fruit for influencing your realm for the Kingdom of God (ministry). When you deny your old self, refuse the path that Adam and Eve chose which led to the World's system, you will discover all three types of fruit become manifested in your life.

Adam went from fruit to thorns, now you can go from thorns to fruit!

This would be a great time to just sit back and bask in the presence of God. Once you have gone through the Tabernacle as we have described, take some time here to be quiet and enjoy being with Him. You do not even have to talk. God enjoys this, and you will too. This is what this lesson is all about, coming into the presence of God! Stop and enjoy God.

Determine that you will practice the presence of God on a daily basis. It is the main ingredient for victory in this life and the next.

End Notes

[i] Nee, Watchman. A Table in the Wilderness. Wheaton, IL: Tyndale House, 1965

[ii] Nee, Watchman. God's Plan and The Overcomers. Wheaton, IL: Tyndale House, 1979

Made in the USA
Charleston, SC
22 June 2011